Adviser Essentials
Project Planning

Lyn Fiscus

supporting positive youth development

Leadership Logistics

11086 Glade Ct., Reston, VA 20191-4715

703-860-2259

info@leadershiplogistics.us

www.leadershiplogistics.us

Contents

Chapter 4: Keeping Project Files

Preface

Project planning skills are among the skills students learn in student activities that will stay with them for life. I hear from students I had in leadership class more than 20 years ago that the skills they learned planning our activities are ones they continue to use in all facets of their adult lives. When I think back to those early days of advising, I didn't really have any idea that what I was teaching them was so valuable. Like most student activity advisers, I got the job with no prior training on how to work with a student organization. My school had a very active student council, with a full slate of activities that were traditionally done, and as the adviser I was expected to make it all happen. I spent a lot of time *doing* before I realized that my main role was *advising*.

A veteran adviser who read this book for me before publication pointed out that most advisers don't use forms and checklists like the ones in this book with their student leaders. It's easier to just tell the students what to do or do things yourself. But either of those options overlooks the important role of student activities in education. Yes, it takes more time to teach students how to plan a project and carry it out than to just do it yourself. But doing it yourself or telling students how to do it leaves students no better off than they were before you started. Teaching them the process of planning the activity provides them with thinking skills they will be able to use in many situations.

And that's where this book comes in. The information and forms in this book can be used as a tool to help plan your organization's activities. By sharing them with student leaders and making the use of these materials part of your project planning routine, you will be teaching your students a transferable skill that will make their participation in your organization an integral part of their education. Whatever they end up doing as adults—from running a business to serving as a volunteer on their local PTA—the ability to break a project down into the steps that need to be accomplished, prioritize them, and pull all the elements together to make the project happen is invaluable. I encourage you to take the time to teach the process.

Sincerely,

Lyn Fiscus

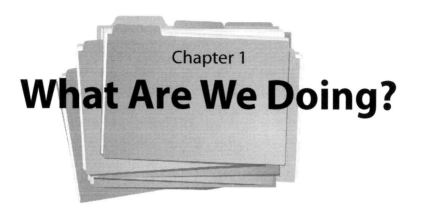

Chapter 1

What Are We Doing?

In This Chapter

- Generating Project Ideas
- Creating the Plan
- Backwards Planning

- Project Budgets
- Project Approval
- Standardizing the Process

Project planning is the backbone of most student activity groups. Aside from meeting skills, student leaders use project-planning skills most often to carry out the work of their organization. While every project is different, basically three kinds of information are needed when planning an activity:

- What needs to be done?
- Who is going to do it?
- When must it be completed?

Although each project has many specific details that make the event unique, the steps involved in planning the projects are usually similar. Keeping in mind the basics of what needs to be done, who needs to do it, and when it needs to be done will help any student leader successfully manage project planning.

Generating Project Ideas

Everything begins with an idea. Someone has an idea for a project, or an event comes up on the school calendar that your group has always been responsible for, and your members start asking, "What should we do for _____ this year?" If you've ever noticed that the activities your organization sponsors tend to be the same from year to year—oh sure, you might have a different theme for a dance, or sell ghost lollygrams instead of pumpkin-shaped ones at Halloween, but usually there are only minor twists on old ideas—you might want to invest some effort in creative brainstorming.

Sky's the Limit Brainstorming

Ever had a brainstorming session that was more of a gentle rain than a storm? Generating creativity on demand isn't easy, so you need to prime the pump for a good brainstorming session. To do this, begin with a little exercise that has nothing to do with the task at hand but that will get people thinking beyond the usual. For example, before brainstorming for themes for an upcoming dance, take five minutes and ask your group members to come up with all the ways life would be different if we had two thumbs on each hand—or if animals could talk, or if our elbows bent the other way, or any oddball question. It's kind of goofy, but once people start thinking about the question they'll come up with many unusual ideas. You can segue into a brainstorming session on an upcoming project by saying something like "These are great ideas. Now how can we apply that same creativity to making our dance theme something fun and different?"

Another technique that can stimulate out-of-the-box thinking is to change the normal parameters for a project. Ask members to pretend for a few minutes that the budget for an upcoming project is $100,000. With that kind of money, what could you do? Many outrageous ideas are bound to be mentioned, but write them all down. Using

Mind Map—Snowcoming Spirit Week

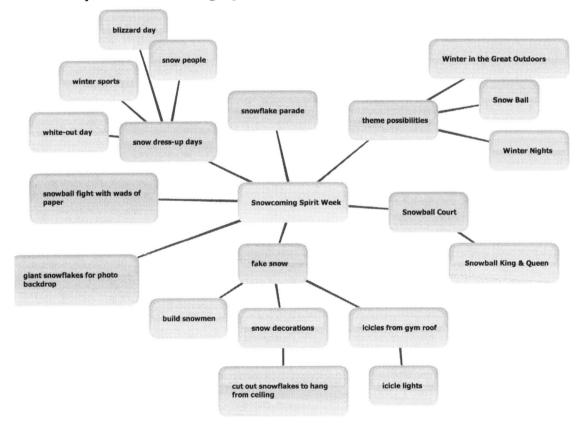

a mind map is a good way to help people build on others' ideas and link related items. (Check online for free mind-mapping software like that found at *www.bubbl.us*, which was used for the sample mind map on page 2.) After members have gotten all their ideas out, take a look at what is listed and ask them to come up with ways that these impractical ideas could be tweaked into something usable. For example, instead of having a celebrity at the event, how about having a celebrity look-alike contest? Or, instead of a famous band, what about an air-band contest or a lip-synch contest? Instead of hiring a skywriter to write a message to publicize an event, how about a radio-controlled model airplane pulling a banner around the parking lot after school? Ask yourselves, "What can we do with little or no budget that would be like this expensive idea?"

Borrow with a Twist

While we're on the subject of adapting ideas, consider all the ways you can adapt things that are popular in our culture right now and convert them into successful activities at your school. Television shows are a goldmine of ideas for activities.

- How about sponsoring a [Your School] Idol contest instead of the tired old talent show?

- Do a take-off of *The Amazing Race* for a class competition during spirit week.

- Pair students with staff members to have a dance-off similar to the *Dancing with the Stars* television show.

- Get a couple of teachers to agree to trade classrooms and do a *Trading Spaces*-style redecorating.

- Have an *Iron Chef* cook-off between faculty members or coaches.

- Organize an evening of game shows with students or faculty members as contestants. Have teachers make up questions for a *Jeopardy*-type quiz show or a take-off on *Who Wants to Be a Millionaire* or *Are You Smarter than a Fifth Grader?* Survey your student body and do a version of *Family Feud* with spirit points instead of dollar amounts.

Advertising is another element of popular culture that can be mined for ideas. Millions of dollars are spent each year by Madison Avenue marketing firms to research what works so they can produce more effective ads. Take a lesson from what works for them and see if you can adapt a successful campaign to work for your activity. Don't copy trademarked or copyrighted campaigns, but consider what makes the ads appealing or effective, and strive to replicate the look or feel of the original by translating it into words and images that work for your activity.

Another good way to get new ideas is to check out what other schools are doing. There are a variety of ways to do this:

Attend workshops. If you have an opportunity to attend a district, state, or national workshop or conference, take it! These meetings are excellent chances to learn about what others are doing and pick up new ideas.

Check out websites. Many student activity groups and other organizations have websites on which they post project ideas from members. Surfing the pages of these sites is bound to give you some new ideas:

• **ASB Director: Student Activities Resource**. From Homecoming Week to Prom, and everything in between, this site covers it all with free tips and ideas for planning events and fundraisers. *www. asbdirector.com*

• **Student council websites.** The National Association of Student Councils has an extensive listing of project ideas gleaned from active councils around the country under the "Student Council Project Ideas" tab on its website at *www.nasc.us.*

State student council association sites also often have idea exchange sections, although the quality of information varies considerably from state to state. The Michigan site (*http://mascmahs.org/idea*) and the Washington site (*www.awsp.org/Content/awsp/ StudentLeadership/Resources/default.htm*) are two of the more useful ones. A listing of all the state websites can be found on the National Association of State Student Council Executive Directors (NASSCED) website at *www.nassced.org/directory/whoweare.html*

• **Canadian Association of Student Activity Advisors.** Go north of the border for some ideas with a Canadian twist. Polar Express Parade, Tinman Triathalon, and Watermelon Carving Contest are just a few of the unique ideas found here. Visit *www. casaaleadership.ca/CASAAswapshop.html*

• **DifferenceMakers.** The Swap Shop section of this site has a number of ideas for activities. Visit *www.differencemakers.com/ swapshop/swapshop_main.html*

Sometimes just making students aware that it's good to do things differently can stimulate more creativity. When everyone knows "that's the way we've always done it" isn't necessarily the right way or the best way, you'll be amazed at the innovative ideas that may start bubbling up as your group members work to put their own creative stamp on group activities.

Creating the Plan

You've done your group brainstorming and selected a project. Everyone loves the idea and votes to proceed. Great. Now, what do you do?

Purpose

First, determine your purpose in sponsoring this project. A student organization shouldn't sponsor any project just to do it, or just because it's always been done. Projects are not goals in and of themselves, merely the methods by which you will accomplish your broader goals. Every project should support the goals of your organization. (See Project Planning Overview on page 10.) For example, sponsoring the Homecoming dance could support a goal of cultivating a positive school climate; hosting a breakfast for the faculty could support a goal of improving faculty-student relations; producing a multimedia slideshow at the end of the year could support a goal of involving every student, and so forth. If a proposed project doesn't support one of your group's goals, then perhaps another activity would make better use of your time and efforts.

Goals

Once you know the purpose of your project, it's a good idea to set some specific project goals you hope to achieve. To set a goal, define it in a clear, precise statement that has the following:

- It is realistic and achievable, but provides a challenge.
- It has measurable results (i.e., you can tell whether it has been accomplished or not).
- It is clear, specific, and understandable.
- You are responsible for whether it happens or not (i.e., it doesn't depend on someone else to happen).
- It is beneficial.
- It has a deadline for completion.

How will you determine whether or not a project was successful? This will relate directly to your purpose and goals for the activity. In the case of the multimedia presentation, perhaps you want to include a photo of every student and teacher in the school. Or include photos of every major event during the year as a flashback. Or involve non-members by reaching out to students in the

school's photography classes or computer classes. If those are your measures of success, your specific goals might be stated:

- We will include a photo of every student and teacher.
- We will involve non-members by asking the photography club to help take photos.
- We will include three photos of every major event from the school year.

If you need help figuring out the goals for your project, ask yourselves:

- Why are we sponsoring this activity?
- What do we hope to accomplish by having this activity?
- How will we know if we have done what we set out to do?

Backwards Planning

With your purpose and goals in mind, now comes the task of imagining what the final product will be. To borrow a phrase from Steven Covey, "Begin with the end in mind." Brainstorm what the project will look like, sound like, and feel like when it is completed, then list all the tasks that need to be done to accomplish that vision.

For example, if your group had a goal of promoting positive faculty-student relations, you might plan to host an appreciation lunch for faculty and staff members on an in-service training day. Group members may envision a nicely decorated cafeteria where faculty and staff members sit at tables after going through a buffet line with a variety of delectable food choices. Student leaders serve beverages at the tables and bus tables as staff members finish eating. A multimedia presentation of candid photos of teachers and staff members doing their work plays continuously on one wall, accompanied by inspirational music.

Ask yourself: *What will it take to make this happen?* Work backwards from what you envision and break the project down into steps that will enable you to accomplish it. In this example, several discrete elements can be broken out:

Decorations. To achieve the objective of having a nicely decorated cafeteria you must determine what decorations you want and obtain them. If you plan to order them from a catalog, determine how much time is needed to get a purchase order, place the order, and have the decorations shipped to you. Back up from the date of the faculty lunch and set a deadline for ordering the decorations that will ensure they arrive in time. You will also need to recruit and schedule people to help decorate the cafeteria before the lunch.

Food. To achieve the objective of having a variety of delectable food choices you must determine what type of food you want and how you will obtain it. Will it be a catered event? If so, you will need to secure a caterer and go through the necessary steps of checking prices, getting a contract, getting a check to pay the caterer, and so forth. Will you have students bring in homemade dishes? If so, you will need to create a sign-up sheet with the various types of food—salad, side dish, main course, dessert, bread, etc.— and have members sign up to bring a dish. Whichever method you choose, determine how much time each of these steps will take. Plan backwards from the date of the event and schedule deadlines by which you must accomplish each step.

PowerPoint presentation. To achieve the objective of having a motivational PowerPoint presentation of candid photos of staff members, you must set dates by which members will take photos, select and obtain the music that will accompany the presentation, and put the show together. You must also submit requests for the necessary audio/visual equipment.

Servers. To achieve the objective of having student servers at the event, you must recruit students to help, devise a schedule, and assign people to work at the various stations you need.

Invitations. To achieve the objective of having faculty and staff members attend the event, you must let them know about it. Will you put an announcement in the faculty bulletin? If so, what is the deadline for submitting the announcement? Will you create individual invitations or send an e-mail invitation? If so, when do you plan to put them in teacher mailboxes or send the e-mail? Back up from that target date and give yourself time to create a design, obtain supplies, get them made or photocopied, or create the digital invitation. Who will do each job?

Project Budgets

Part of figuring out what your activity will entail is calculating how much it's all going to cost. It's important for each project your organization sponsors to operate within a budget. Without a guideline of how much money is available for the project, it's easy to go overboard on expenses. For example, the Spring Fling committee might like to spend money on leis, tropical decorations, and free pineapple drinks for everyone who attends, but without first estimating how much money the Spring Fling mixer is likely to bring in, they won't know if they have the money to do what they plan.

Follow these steps to create a project budget:

Look at previous expenses and income as a guide. If the event has been held before, check organization files to see how many people attended and what the expenses were. If it's a new event, estimate expenses and income from similar events, or make your best guess. Be sure to account for increased costs because of inflation.

Estimate revenue. How much money will the activity likely bring in? Use the form on page 14 to help you consider all sources of revenue, including ticket sales (advance and at the door), concessions, ad revenue from programs, donations, and so forth. As part of estimating ticket sales, calculate how many people can be expected to participate in the activity; you also will need this figure for estimating expenses.

Estimate expenses. Use the form on page 12 and consider all the areas in which your group will have expenses.

- Will refreshments be served? If so, figure costs for the food and drink and also cups, napkins, plates, etc.

- What publicity costs are involved? Will you need to buy poster-making supplies, run off fliers, print tickets, make programs?

- Will there be rental fees for the site or equipment?

- Are decorations needed? If so, list each item and its cost.

- Will there be contracted entertainment, such as a DJ?

- Will there be prizes or awards? Sometimes donations can be obtained for these, but if you are awarding ribbons or plaques, the cost must be factored in.

- How will you thank people who have helped with the event? The cost of flowers or a fruit basket for a faculty member who really helped, or small candy bars to accompany thank-you notes should be part of the budget.

Compare estimated expenses with estimated revenue. For most projects, you want your revenue figures to be higher than your expenses. If they are not, you have two options. Either figure out how to trim expenses so they are in line with revenue, or figure out how to increase the revenue for the project (e.g., raising the ticket price, seeking donations for needed supplies, or selling ads for a program).

Occasionally, you will have projects that are

worthwhile and advance the mission of your organization but they don't bring in enough revenue to pay for themselves. In these cases, you must look for ways to make a profit elsewhere.

Project Approval

Gaining approval to go ahead with your project will depend on the procedures in place at your school. If the project has been done before, often this is just a formality, a matter of getting a form signed and adding the event to the school calendar. Sometimes you will need to prepare a presentation to a principal or other administrator to receive approval.

If you or your students need to present a project to an administrator for approval, follow these guidelines:

- Prepare a written summary of what the project will entail and key points you want to cover.

- Make an appointment with the administrator's secretary. If copies of information would be helpful to the administrator before the meeting, give the copies to the secretary with a note indicating that "this will be useful for the meeting."

- Be prepared to answer questions about any part of your proposal. Anticipate concerns the administrator might have and be ready to explain how the concerns will be addressed.

- Practice the presentation, with someone playing the role of the administrator.

- Be on time (or early) and bring all materials you might need.

- Cover all areas of your proposal, its advantages and disadvantages.

- Listen carefully to the administrator's questions and concerns; address them honestly. Be willing to incorporate suggestions that will allow the project to proceed.

- Write up an accurate report of the meeting, date it, and file it. Send a copy of the report to the principal with a thank-you note for taking the time to meet with you.

- Assess whether you achieved your purposes and what you would do differently next time. If needed, revise and try again.

The 12 Ws of Project Planning

WHAT are you planning to do?

WHY do you want to do this project?

WHEN will the event occur?

WHERE will the activity take place?

WHO will benefit from the project?

WHAT approvals will be needed?

WHAT funds are needed?

WHAT will it take to make this happen?

WHAT committees are necessary?

WHAT type of publicity is needed?

WHO deserves a special thank-you?

WHAT follow-up is needed?

Standardizing the Process

How can you put this project planning process in place for each project you organize? In general, it's useful to go through the 12 Ws of Project Planning (see box on page 8) to begin organizing your thoughts. Using checklists such as the General Checklist for Activity Planning (pg. 15) and standardized forms such as the Project Planning form (pg. 17), Publicity Planning form (page 19), Event Budget Worksheets (pages 12–14), and Task Assignment Sheet (page 28) will help student leaders work through some of the usual tasks that are common to all projects and encourage them to consider aspects they might not think of on their own. By making these forms part of your project planning routine, student leaders will begin to develop their own expertise at project planning.

Project Planning Overview

What goals have we decided to accomplish this year?

1. _____

2. _____

3. _____

4. _____

5. _____

What projects will achieve these goals?

August

Project: _____ # Goal to which it relates: _____

Project: _____ # Goal to which it relates: _____

September

Project: _____ # Goal to which it relates: _____

Project: _____ # Goal to which it relates: _____

October

Project: _____ # Goal to which it relates: _____

Project: _____ # Goal to which it relates: _____

November

Project: _____ # Goal to which it relates: _____

Project: _____ # Goal to which it relates: _____

December

Project: _____ # Goal to which it relates: _____

Project: _____ # Goal to which it relates: _____

January

Project: _____ # Goal to which it relates: _____

Project: _____ # Goal to which it relates: _____

February

Project: _____ # Goal to which it relates: _____

Project: _____ # Goal to which it relates: _____

March

Project: _____ # Goal to which it relates: _____

Project: _____ # Goal to which it relates: _____

April

Project: _____ # Goal to which it relates: _____

Project: _____ # Goal to which it relates: _____

May

Project: _____ # Goal to which it relates: _____

Project: _____ # Goal to which it relates: _____

June

Project: _____ # Goal to which it relates: _____

Project: _____ # Goal to which it relates: _____

Event Budget Worksheet — Part 1: Expenses

Name of Event: _____

Estimate the expenses you will incur in the following areas for the event you are planning. After the event, fill in the actual amounts and file this form in the project file for future reference.

Site	Estimated	Actual	Notes
Room and hall fees	_____	_____	
Custodial staff	_____	_____	
Equipment	_____	_____	
Tables and chairs	_____	_____	
Security	_____	_____	
Other	_____	_____	
Subtotals:	_____	_____	

Refreshments	Estimated	Actual
Food	_____	_____
Drinks	_____	_____
Utensils	_____	_____
Other	_____	_____
Subtotals:	_____	_____

Publicity	Estimated	Actual
Paint and Paper	_____	_____
Graphics work	_____	_____
Photocoypying/Printing	_____	_____
Postage	_____	_____
Subtotals:	_____	_____

Decorations	Estimated	Actual
Flowers	_____	_____
Lighting/Candles	_____	_____
Balloons	_____	_____
Paper supplies	_____	_____
Streamers	_____	_____
Paint	_____	_____
Other	_____	_____
Subtotals:	_____	_____

Entertainment	Estimated	Actual
DJ or Band	_____	_____
Speaker	_____	_____
Other	_____	_____
Subtotals:	_____	_____

Prizes	Estimated	Actual
Ribbons / Plaques	_____	_____
Gifts	_____	_____
Door prizes	_____	_____
Other	_____	_____
Subtotals:	_____	_____

Miscellaneous	Estimated	Actual
_____	_____	_____
_____	_____	_____
_____	_____	_____
_____	_____	_____
Subtotals:	_____	_____
TOTAL EXPENSES:	_____	_____

Summary of Profit/Loss

Using the information from your expense and revenue worksheets, summarize your event's profit or loss.

	Estimated	Actual
Total income:	_____	_____
Total expenses:	_____	_____
Total profit (or loss):	_____	_____

Event Budget Worksheet — Part 2: Revenue

Estimate the revenue you will generate in the following areas for the event you are planning.

Presale Tickets	Price	Estimated	Actual	Notes
_____ adults @	_____	_____	_____	
_____ children @	_____	_____	_____	
_____ other @	_____	_____	_____	
Subtotals:		_____	_____	

Tickets at the Door	Price	Estimated	Actual
_____ adults @	_____	_____	_____
_____ children @	_____	_____	_____
_____ other @	_____	_____	_____
Subtotals:		_____	_____

Concession Sales	Price	Estimated	Actual
_____ @	_____	_____	_____
_____ @	_____	_____	_____
_____ @	_____	_____	_____
_____ @	_____	_____	_____
_____ @	_____	_____	_____
_____ @	_____	_____	_____
_____ @	_____	_____	_____
Subtotals:		_____	_____

Other Revenue Sources	Estimated	Actual
Advertising sales	_____	_____
Program sales	_____	_____
Other: _____	_____	_____
Other: _____	_____	_____
Other: _____	_____	_____
Other: _____	_____	_____
Subtotals:	_____	_____
TOTAL REVENUE:	_____	_____

General Checklist for Activity Planning

The steps involved in planning an activity will vary depending on the type of activity. Review the following list and check the items needed for your event.

Name of Event: _____

Administrative

❏ Obtain administrative approval for the activity

❏ Put the activity date on the school calendar

❏ Make arrangements to reserve needed facilities (gym, cafeteria, etc.)

❏ Submit requests for custodial assistance

    ❏ Chairs   ❏ Tables

    ❏ Risers   ❏ Podium

    ❏ Trash cans   ❏ Other:

Audio/Visual needs

❏ Microphone

❏ Sound system

❏ Lights (spotlight, stage lights, etc.)

❏ Projector (LCD, slide, movie, etc.)

❏ MP3 or CD player

❏ Other:

Decorations

❏ Select theme

❏ Order decorations

❏ Organize people to decorate

❏ Gather supplies for decorating: tape, scissors, air pumps, staplers, trash cans, etc.

Tickets

❏ Determine admission/ticket price

❏ Design ticket

❏ Arrange for tickets to be printed

❏ Schedule ticket sales workers

❏ Arrange for cash box for ticket sales

❏ Arrange for depositing money from sales

Publicity

❏ Design and create posters, fliers, table tents

❏ Create PA announcements

❏ Draft press release and deliver to local media

❏ Send invitations to special guests

❏ Alert yearbook/newspaper staff to have a photographer at the event

❏ Other:

Program

❏ Create schedule of events

❏ Contract with entertainment (band/DJ, speaker, games equipment, etc.)

❏ Request checks to pay for contracted services (band/DJ, security, caterer, etc.)

❏ Schedule rehearsal

❏ Design printed program

❏ Arrange for program to be printed

❏ Determine program distribution method (on chairs, hand out, etc.) and recruit workers

Refreshments

❏ Order refreshments or contract with caterer

❏ Arrange for ice, tables, etc., for refreshments

❏ Obtain necessary supplies: cups, plates, napkins, eating utensils, serving utensils, etc.

❏ Organize servers for refreshment distribution

❏ Arrange for a cash box if selling refreshments

Chaperones/Security

❏ Request administrative supervision

❏ Recruit chaperones

❏ Create a schedule of work stations and list of duties for chaperones

❏ Create chart for layout of event and traffic flow

❏ Create a token of appreciation for chaperones or write thank-you notes

❏ Hire security guards for parking lot patrol

Judging/Contests

❏ Determine criteria for judging

❏ Recruit judges

❏ Create judging sheets

❏ Determine and obtain prizes

❏ Write thank-you notes to judges

Follow Up

❏ Organize clean-up effort

❏ Conduct evaluation

❏ Write and send thank-you notes

❏ Complete reports for the files

General Planning Notes:

Project Planning

Name of Project:_____

Chairperson: _____ Overall goal this project supports:_____

Date, time, location of project:_____

Purpose of project: ◯ Tradition ◯ Social ◯ Service ◯ Spirit ◯ Fundraiser ◯ Other

Visualize the project as you would like it to be. What will it consist of?

_____

_____

_____

List three goals you want to achieve with this project.

1. _____

2. _____

3 _____

Checklist: Do you need any of the following? If so, describe on the back of this form.

◯ Administrative approval
◯ Master calendar request
◯ Facility request
◯ Custodial arrangements
◯ Legal contracts
◯ Check requests
◯ Cash box
◯ Tickets
◯ Chaperones/Security
◯ Judges

◯ Prizes
◯ Special guest invitations
◯ Audio/visual equipment
◯ Special equipment
◯ Set-up/clean-up crew
◯ Work schedule
◯ Decorations
◯ Refreshments
◯ Printed program
◯ Other: _____

Publicity: What types of publicity do you need?

○ Posters

○ PA announcements

○ Fliers

○ Table tents

○ Website item

○ E-mails

○ Bulletin boards

○ Press release

○ In-school TV/radio commercial

○ Community access cable

○ Twitter/Facebook/YouTube item

○ Other (be creative!): _____

Budget: How much money do you have to work with? _____

Do you have necessary approval to spend money?   ○ Yes   ○ No

Materials: List all materials or equipment needed.

Item	Source	Cost

Publicity Planning

Event name: _____

Date: _____ Time: _____ Place: _____

Special theme, logo, or colors that should be used: _____

Budget for publicity: _____ Date publicity should begin:_____

Will tickets be needed?   ○ Yes   ○ No

On sale when? _____ On sale where? _____

Ticket price: _____ Sales start: _____ Sales end:_____

What audience do we want to reach?
○ Students   ○ Parents   ○ Faculty/staff   ○ Community   ○ Other

Methods we will use to reach our audiences: Who will be responsible:

○ Bulletin/PA announcements   _____

○ Posters   _____

○ Marquee or electronic message board   _____

○ Fliers   _____

○ Table tents   _____

○ Chalkboard/whiteboard notices   _____

○ Sidewalk chalking   _____

○ Locker signs   _____

○ Yard signs   _____

○ Press release   _____

○ Radio PSAs   _____

○ Website item   _____

○ Blast e-mail or text message   _____

○ YouTube, Facebook, or Twitter item   _____

○ Newsletter item   _____

○ Bulletin board   _____

○ In-school TV/radio ad   _____

○ Community access cable   _____

○ Other (be creative!):   _____

Write any additional information, ideas, or suggestions on the back of this form.

Event Publicity Timeline

Event name: _____

Briefly describe the publicity methods you are using and indicate when they should be implemented.

Two/Three Months Out:

Six Weeks Out:

Four Weeks Out:

Two Weeks Out:

One Week Out:

6 Days Before Event:

5 Days Before Event:

4 Days Before Event:

3 Days Before Event:

2 Days Before Event:

1 Day Before Event:

Day of Event:

Facility Use Checklist

Event Name: _____ Date of Event: _____

Start Time: _____ End Time: _____

Facility Needed: _____

❏ Put the activity date on the school calendar

❏ Reserve needed facilities (gym, cafeteria, etc.)

Custodial/Maintenance Needs

❏ Submit requests for custodial assistance

   ❏ Tables   Type of table: _____   # of tables needed: _____

   ❏ Chairs   Type of chair: _____   # of chairs needed: _____

   ❏ Staging   ❏ Risers   ❏ Podium

❏ Trash cans

❏ Other: _____

Audio/Visual Needs

❏ Microphone

❏ Sound system

❏ Lights (spotlight, stage lights, etc.)

❏ Projector: ❏ LCD   ❏ overhead   ❏ slide   ❏ movie

❏ Screen

❏ TV

❏ DVD player

❏ MP3 or CD player

❏ Other: _____

Room Set-Up

Describe how the room(s) should be set up for this event. Attach a sketch of where items should be located.

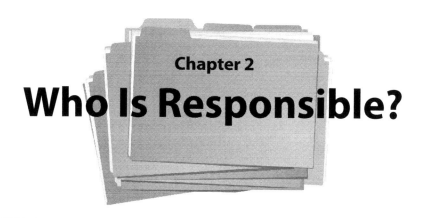

Who Is Responsible?

In This Chapter

The next step to make your project a reality is to determine who will do each of the tasks on the list of all that needs to be accomplished. How many people are needed to get it all done? What skills are necessary? Who will assume responsibility to ensure nothing is overlooked?

Committees Are Vital

At this stage it's usually a good idea to form committees to handle the different types of work and get more people involved. Committees are a vital element in a successful student organization. Committees make big jobs manageable by breaking them into smaller segments and involve more people in the group's activities by assigning people to be responsible for those segments. The result is greater e▨ciency and a stronger group.

Reasons to Form Committees

Wherever and whenever there is a task that can't be handled by one or two people in a short period of time, a committee is likely to be formed. There are many reasons for setting up committees, regardless of the tasks they are to complete. In the earlier example of a faculty appreciation lunch, an overall committee organized to plan the lunch might break up into sub-committees for each of the areas outlined: decorations, food, multimedia presentation, servers, and invitations. Spreading the work out in this manner helps involve more people in the group's activities so they feel ownership in its projects. It also enables your group to use the talent and abilities of a larger group of student leaders and avoid overusing its o▨cers.

Assigning group members to committees where their specialized skills can be used to best advantage makes good use of the resources available to the organization. Committee work is also an excellent opportunity to provide training to younger members of the group so they can gain experience and confidence to serve as officers or chairs when they become upperclassmen.

Finally, a committee can save time for the larger group by discussing and eliminating impractical ideas and by selecting the most relevant, valuable ideas to recommend to the organization for action.

Forming a Committee

Committees are formed for specific purposes and may be used to:

• Brainstorm about a project

• Plan specific activities

• Present the best ideas to the large group

• Investigate issues and report the findings to the large group

• Perform specific work (sell tickets, clean up after a dance, etc.)

• Get more done in less time by delegating responsibilities.

A committee will not work effectively unless all the members know what they are supposed to do and are committed to getting it done. When forming a committee, the following questions should be answered:

• What is the purpose of the committee?

• What are its responsibilities and limitations?

• What are the specific tasks to be accomplished?

• When should the job be completed and what type of report is expected?

• What is the role of officers and how is the membership of the committee to be decided?

• What is the term of office for members, method of filling vacancies, and method for appointing the chair?

• What is the authority of the committee?

• Is there a budget?

• What resources are needed? What resources are already available?

Committee members may be appointed, chosen from volunteers, or elected by the members of the entire group. The committee should be a congenial group, yet represent several points of view. Its size may vary according to the project and the scope of work to be accomplished. Obviously, a committee decorating a hall for a dance will have more members than a committee that is investigating the cost of bands. Smaller groups often work more effectively, although in some situations it is better to have too many people on a committee than too few, as is the case with a committee assigned the job of cleaning up after a school rally.

It's a good idea to keep a written record of a committee's work during meetings and other times (see page 27). This information will be a key part of the project file (see Chapter 4), and will be helpful in remembering who agreed to do what.

Selecting Committee Members

A willingness to serve on a committee and do the work is often the only trait student leaders look for when making up the membership of their committees. Some other traits to look for in committee members include:

• Willingness to consider other points of view

• Willingness to drop an argument for the sake of moving ahead with the bigger issues

• Alert listening and honest questioning

• Ability to think logically

• Talents that mesh with those of other committee members

• Ability to follow through on assignments

• Time management skills.

Committee members also have important responsibilities. Without their dedication, the committee will fail. Good committee members must:

• Know the purpose of the committee

• Understand the specific task they have been assigned

• Attend all the meetings

• Participate in planning, share ideas, ask questions

• Commit to completing their work on time

• Keep track of supplies used, money spent, etc.

• Be respectful of the chairperson and other members

• Keep the full committee up-to-date on the tasks they have been assigned.

How Big Should the Committee Be?

Some general rules about committee size are:

• The ideal size for groups attempting to discuss and develop ideas is between five and seven people. With fewer than five people, the variety of perspectives needed is not available; with more than seven people, members may become frustrated because of the number of others who also want to speak.

• Members of a working committee should have enough to keep busy. People who show up to work on an assignment but find nothing to do may be reluctant to become involved again.

• Members should not be overworked—the quality of their project diminishes, and they may not want to help in the future.

The Committee Chair's Role

Each committee should have a designated leader, someone who has final responsibility for seeing that the work is done. This person should be selected after careful consideration by the organization. Choose someone who is interested and can work easily with others. The chair's role is not necessarily one of bringing technical expertise to the group. The fact that a person is a good artist does not mean that he or she will be good at chairing the publicity committee. The chair must be organized and know how to organize both programs and people. He or she must know how to involve others and motivate them to do the work of the committee. The chairperson must work with the committee members to decide WHAT has to be done, WHO will do it, and WHEN it must be completed.

Resist the temptation to put "ASAP" as the deadline; specific dates are harder to put off when life gets busy and many tasks are being juggled. To set deadlines, work backwards from the date the item is needed and allow enough time to get each item finished. When setting deadlines, always allow yourself a little wiggle room, if possible, to accommodate unforeseen circumstances— ordered decorations get delayed in shipping, equipment breaks down, a key person gets sick, etc.

Writing down these responsibilities and agreements can help ensure that all tasks are assigned to someone and that everyone involved knows what is expected of them and what their deadlines are. Using a form like the Task Assignment Sheet on page 28 can help committees organize the work and ensure that nothing is overlooked. Individuals may find forms like the Delegation Agreement sheet (page 29), the Action Step Planner (page 30) and the Event Day Planner (page 31) to be helpful in organizing their part of the workload.

A Word About Delegating

Good committee leaders don't try to do all the work themselves, but instead delegate responsibilities to members of their committees. When delegating, it's best to focus on the result to be achieved, not the method of achieving it. Let members use their own knowledge and skills to come up with a way to do it—their way might even turn out to be better!

Although leaders may delegate control of certain tasks, they should maintain some responsibility for the outcome. They should check periodically to see how the project is going. It may not be enough to merely ask, "How's the slide show going?" They may need to ask specific questions: "How many photographers have you recruited?" "Have you gotten a list of student names from the office yet?" "What program are you using to put together the show?" "What music have you selected?"

The delegate's ability—or lack of ability—to answer these types of questions will give a good indication of how well the project is progressing.

Committee Report

Name of Committee: _____

Committee Assignment: _____

_____

Key Discussion Points:

Action Items:

Recommendations and/or Points for Further Discussion:

Names of Committee Members Attending Meeting:

Meeting Date: _____ Signature of Chair: _____

Task Assignment Sheet

List each task to be done, who is responsible for completing it, and a deadline for completion.

Task to be completed	Who's doing it?	By when?

Form completed by: _____ Date: _____

Delegation Agreement

Use this worksheet to clarify expectations when delegating a task to a committee member.

What is the project or task being delegated? _____

What must be done for the completion of this task to be considered a success?

When must the task be completed? _____

On what dates will we touch base to check on progress?

    Checkpoint #1 _____

    Checkpoint #2 _____

    Checkpoint #3 _____

How much authority does the person to whom the task is delegated have to act?

    ○ Just do it—we trust your judgment.

    ○ Create a plan and run it by the adviser before acting.

    ○ Get approval for every step of the process.

Who should be consulted if help is needed or questions arise while completing this task?

    ○ Adviser _____

    ○ President _____

    ○ Committee chair _____

    ○ Other _____

Person assigning the task: _____ Person taking on the task: _____

Action Step Planner

Task to be completed: _____ Deadline: _____

Action steps I will take to complete this task:

1. _____

2. _____

3. _____

4. _____

Task to be completed: _____ Deadline: _____

Action steps I will take to complete this task:

1. _____

2. _____

3. _____

4. _____

Task to be completed: _____ Deadline: _____

Action steps I will take to complete this task:

1. _____

2. _____

3. _____

4. _____

Task to be completed: _____ Deadline: _____

Action steps I will take to complete this task:

1. _____

2. _____

3. _____

4. _____

Event Day Planner

Event: _____ Date of Event: _____

Location: _____ Time of Event: _____

	Tasks to be accomplished:	**Notes:**
7:00 a.m.		
8:00 a.m.		
9:00 a.m.		
10:00 a.m.		
11:00 a.m.		
12:00 p.m.		
1:00 p.m.		
2:00 p.m.		
3:00 p.m.		
4:00 p.m.		
5:00 p.m.		
6:00 p.m.		
7:00 p.m.		
8:00 p.m.		

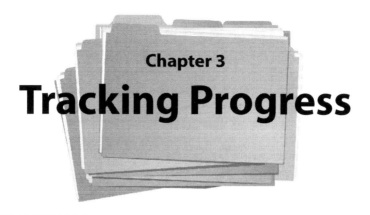

Chapter 3

Tracking Progress

In This Chapter

- Task Assignment Sheets
- Activity Duty Charts
- Project Planning Tree

- Gantt Charts
- Oversized Timelines
- Project Planning Tree Form

When tackling all the myriad tasks involved in planning student activities—trying to keep track of who is doing what, when they are supposed to have it completed, how much it's all going to cost—it's easy to sometimes overlook details and let something slip through the cracks. A variety of methods are available for keeping details from being overlooked.

Task Assignment Sheets

One of the simplest methods of keeping track of all these details is to list all the tasks, assignments, and deadlines on a standard form such as the Task Assignment Sheet mentioned in Chapter Two (see page 28). Committee chairs, officers, and the adviser can refer to the sheet to refresh their memory of any details. Use a Task Assignment

Summary sheet (page 38) to keep track of what jobs have been assigned to various committee members.

Activity Duty Charts

A more visual method of tracking details is to create a duty chart based on the brainstormed list of all the tasks that need to be completed. After each committee generates its list of tasks, student leaders assign due dates and "person responsible" names to each task. The committee chair or other designated leader creates a large chart with all the information listed and hangs the chart in the activity room or adviser's room where all can see it.

As a task is completed, the student responsible for it initials the chart. Advisers, officers, and any interested person can easily see the progress of a project by following what tasks have been signed off on. If a deadline has been missed, an officer or the adviser can follow up with the person responsible to address any problems before they become impossible to overcome.

The charts can be saved as reference material for the following year, or the items on them can be transcribed into the final committee report.

Project Planning Trees

Similar in nature to a family tree, a Project Planning Tree starts with a central theme and branches out into sub-categories. The tree provides the main category and the branches show the details within that category.

To create the tree, students generate a list of tasks to be completed and write each task on a sticky note.

Discuss how these fit into categories. Logical planning categories to use are Who, What, and When. As a group, determine which tree format is most appropriate for the project you are planning—should it be a Who tree, a What tree, or a When tree? If the tree is the "who" then the branches will indicate the "what" and the "when." If the tree is the "what" then the branches need to indicate

---

Sample Project Planning Tree

The Project: _Bowl-a-thon_   The Tree: _WHO_   Date Created: _3/24/10_

Branch	Branch	Branch	Branch	Branch	Branch	Branch
Juan	Alaina	Paul	David	Mr. Allen	Madelyn	Adam
Design and copy pledge sheets (4/1)	Contact 2 businesses for prizes (3/25)	Press release for news (3/25)	Contact 2 businesses for prizes (3/25)	Arrange for participants early release (3/20)	Design T-shirts (4/1)	Arrange for ticket sales (3/27)
Arrange for publicity (3/27)	Arrange for sign-up (4/4)	Reserve lanes at bowling alley (3/25)	Order T-shirts (4/5)	Order cash box (4/5)		Get tickets printed (3/30)

the "when" and the "who." (See sample of a Who tree on page 34.)

Organize the sticky notes on a large piece of chart paper and hang it in a place where it can be seen frequently. As tasks are completed, an X may be drawn across the appropriate sticky note. When the total project is completed, the tree may be used in evaluation and the contents of the sticky notes recorded in the committee report for future reference.

Gantt Charts

Invented in the early 1900s by a mechanical engineer named Henry Gantt, a Gantt chart is a timeline in graph form that shows how your work is progressing. In a Gantt chart, dates run along the top of the chart and each task to be performed is written on a separate row with an additional column identifying who is responsible for its completion. Tasks can be grouped by committee or can be listed chronologically.

Each task has a start date, the time required to complete the task, and an end date. A horizontal bar represents the expected timeline for each task, with the left end marking the beginning of the task and the right end marking the expected completion date. As the project progresses, the chart is updated by filling in the bars to a length proportional to the fraction of work that has been done.

Student leaders and the adviser can get a quick status report by drawing a vertical line through the chart at the current date. Completed tasks lie to the left of the line and are completely filled in. Current tasks cross the line and are behind schedule if their filled-in section is to the left of the line and ahead of schedule if the filled-in section stops to the right of the line. Future tasks lie completely to the right of the line.

To be effective, Gantt charts should be limited to 15–20 items so the chart fits on a single page. If the number of tasks is more than 20, break it into separate charts, perhaps listing each committee's work on a separate chart.

There is a wealth of information available online about how to create a Gantt chart, as well as samples and free templates for use in Microsoft Excel. Search online for "Gantt chart template" to find these resources.

Oversized Timelines

To create an oversized timeline, begin with your Task Assignment Sheet listing the tasks to be completed, who is responsible for them, and the dates by which to be completed. On a large sheet of butcher paper, create a weekly or daily timeline—it might start out as a weekly timeline and switch to a daily timeline as you get closer to the event—and list all the tasks in their appropriate place according to their deadline for completion. (See sample on page 36.) Include under each task the person who is responsible for completing it. Post the timeline in the activity room or adviser's room where all can see it. As tasks are completed, the person responsible should check them off and initial to signify they are finished.

Sample Oversized Timeline

Week of 3/21	Week of 3/29	Week of 4/5	Week of 4/12
Contact 3 businesses for prizes *Alaina & David*	Type and copy pledge sheets *Juan*	Order T-shirts *Ben*	Pick up cash box *Mr. Allen*
Press release for news *Paul*	Arrange for sign-up *Alaina*	Order cash box *Mr. Allen*	Pick up prizes from businesses *Alaina & David*
Arrange for participants early release *Mr. Allen*	Design T-shirts *Madelyn*		
Reserve lanes at bowling alley *Paul*	Get tickets printed *Adam*		

The visible nature of this timeline will help keep everyone accountable for what they are supposed to do. If your group doesn't have a place to hang an oversized timeline, create a smaller version on a piece of legal-sized paper and give a copy to everyone in the group. Be sure to transfer the information from the timeline into your final report on the project for the project file.

Developing a method of tracking the progress of a project and using it consistently will enable your group to rest assured that they won't be scrambling around at the last minute trying to make up for a task that was overlooked.

Project Planning Tree

The Project: _____ The Tree : _____ Date Created: _____

Branch	Branch	Branch	Branch	Branch	Branch	Branch

Task Assignment Summary

Project Title: _____

Summarize below the tasks that have been assigned to various committee members for this project.

Member:_____   Contact # _____

Task

Due by   Done?

_____   _____ ❑

_____   _____ ❑

_____   _____ ❑

_____   _____ ❑

Member:_____   Contact # _____

Task

Due by   Done?

_____   _____ ❑

_____   _____ ❑

_____   _____ ❑

_____   _____ ❑

Member:_____   Contact # _____

Task

Due by   Done?

_____   _____ ❑

_____   _____ ❑

_____   _____ ❑

_____   _____ ❑

Member:_____   Contact # _____

Task

Due by   Done?

_____   _____ ❑

_____   _____ ❑

_____   _____ ❑

_____   _____ ❑

Chapter 4
Keeping Project Files

Busy advisers often find themselves lamenting the fact that they are overextended. It seems that good intentions to limit the number of projects taken on fall by the wayside when a great idea comes along, or students plead that "no one else will sponsor this!" Advisers often think, "I can handle one more thing."

You can handle one more thing if you keep in mind that YOU are not the one who should be doing the planning and organizing. You are the adviser, and in that role, you offer guidance, support, and direction so that student leaders can learn from planning and implementing student activities. One thing that can be an immense asset in helping students plan activities is to keep project files of the activities your organization sponsors so your student leaders don't

need to reinvent the wheel every year.

Creating the File

It's a good idea to get into the practice of creating a file for each project and having committee chairs and officers contribute to it. Items that are in any way related to planning and carrying out the activity should be included, such as:

- A project timeline—when to do what

- Committee assignments and a breakdown of areas of responsibility for members

- Number of participants and total work-hours expended

- Copies of purchase orders and contracts

- Copies of correspondence, letters, memos

- Supply lists and sources

- Work order requests for custodial staff

- Sketches of set-up directions for tables, staging, etc.

- People involved and their contact information

- Samples of publicity, announcements, tickets, and programs

- Any communication with the faculty such as excused lists, special bell schedules, etc.

- Evaluation form that identifies problems encountered and recommendations for improvement. (See form on page 41.)

Any items that help provide an overview of the event or program should also be included, such as:

- Photos taken at the event to show decorations, set-up, etc.

- Copies of newspaper articles about the event

- Thank-you notes received

- Committee reports.

Develop an expectation that committee chairs will be responsible for compiling the files. After an event or activity, require the committee chairs and officers to complete a Project Evaluation form (page 41) to add to the file along with any pertinent documentation. Committee members can contribute their perspective and suggestions for improvement by using the Project Evaluation—Committee Members form (page 43).

Set a deadline for completion of the file within two weeks of the end of the project. Offer an incentive or reward for completing the file or include it in the student's grade if it is part of a leadership class. Keep the files in a filing cabinet or other space that students can have access to.

Using the Files

When your organization decides to sponsor an activity, the newly selected or appointed chairpeople should first check the files to see what previous committees have done. If that particular activity hasn't been done before, checking files of similar projects can also provide guidance. New chairs don't have to do the project the same way—they should be encouraged to put their own creative stamp on it—but checking to see what has been done in the past helps them avoid potential pitfalls and build on the successes of their predecessors.

Project Evaluation

Project Title: _____

Date(s) of Project: _____

Brief Description of Project: _____

How would you rate the success of this project? ❏ Outstanding ❏ Good ❏ Needs Improvement

What goals did the project achieve? _____

How many people are needed to do the work to organize this project? _____

How many people attended or participated in this project? _____

Attach a sheet listing the income from this project. Total income: _____

Attach a sheet listing the expenses incurred for this project. Total expenses: _____

Subtract expenses from income to calculate profit: _____

When should planning begin? How much time is needed to prepare and carry out this project? Briefly indicate a timeline for planning this project.

One month before:

Two weeks before:

One week before:

Two days before:

One day before:

Day of event:

What problems did you encounter in planning this project and how were they resolved?

List the aspects of the project that you would do again:

Describe the aspects of the project that should be changed or improved next time it is held:

Other comments or suggestions for future chairs of this event:

Attach a list of all people, businesses, or groups who need thank-you notes.

Project ☐ Should ☐ Should Not be on next year's calendar. Why?

Attach additional information such as supply orders, work requests for custodians, receipts, programs, planning sheets, worker duties, announcement requests, and so forth that may be helpful to the next chairperson of this project.

Evaluation completed by: _____

Project Evaluation—Committee Member

Project Title: _____

Your Name: _____

Description of project:

What specifically did you do to help this project be a success? List everything. Use the back of this sheet if necessary. (Points will be assigned by adviser and committee chairs.)

What suggestions do you have for making this activity better in the future? Include problems you saw and potential solutions.

Committee Member Points: _____/50 pts

Adviser Comments:

About the Author

Lyn Fiscus has been active in the field of student activities for nearly three decades. Her involvement has evolved from active advising to publishing and presenting about student activities.

Lyn taught at the high school level in the St. Louis area for 12 years—10 of those years as a leadership class teacher—and worked with a variety of student groups including student council, yearbook, newspaper, SADD, TREND, pep club, cheerleaders, and American Youth Foundation (AYF) Leadership Compact. She served as assistant director of the Missouri Association of Student Councils (MASC) summer leadership workshop, represented the St. Louis area on the MASC Executive Board for six years, and served on staff of NASSP's National Leadership Camps, becoming co-director of the NLC in New York. In addition, she served as a staff member of AYF's International Leadership Camp for four years, is a former executive board member of the National Association of Student Activity Advisers, and is a frequent presenter at student activities conferences. She was instrumental in the founding of the Alliance for Student Activities, a nonprofit association to promote the value of student activities, and she serves as its vice president.

Lyn was the editor of the award-winning *Leadership for Student Activities*, published by NASSP for student council and National Honor Society advisers, from 1995–2007. She also served as editor of DECA's *Dimensions* magazine from 2006 to 2009, and was editorial consultant for FCCLA's *Teen Times* magazine from 2005 to 2010. She has worked with the Technology Student Association (TSA), SkillsUSA, Herff Jones, Inc., National Middle School Association (NMSA), the National Association of Workshop Directors (NAWD), the California Association of Directors of Activities (CADA), National Organizations for Youth Safety (NOYS), and state student council organizations in Texas, Pennsylvania, Oregon, Michigan, Indiana, and Wisconsin. She currently manages Leadership Logistics, a company she founded in 2004, which provides writing, editing, training, and publishing services to support positive youth development.

Lyn is the author of *Adviser's Guide to Student Activities* (2004) and *Who Says You Can't Change the World* (1991). She served as editor/writer of the *National Leadership Camp Leadership Curriculum Guide* (1994) is co-author of *The Bucks Start Here: Fundraising for Student Activities* (2007) with Earl Reum, and is the founder of the Leadership Teacher website (2009).

In 2005, she was the national recipient of the Earl Reum Award, given by the National Association of Workshop Directors (NAWD) in recognition of outstanding leadership and commitment to the promotion of excellence in student activities. She lives in Reston, Virginia, with her husband and two children.

Also Available from Leadership Logistics

The Adviser's Guide to Student Activities by Lyn Fiscus offers guidance for the new activity adviser on how to work with a student organization. Chapters on getting started, organizing the work, meeting management, financial management, evaluation, and recognition provide strategies and tools to help make the advising role go smoothly. (54 pages) $9.95 plus S/H

The Bucks $tart Here: Fundraising for Student Activities, by Lyn Fiscus and Earl Reum, offers hundreds of ideas for fundraising projects and sales that will put the fun back in fundraising. Try activities like an airband contest, dancing with the staff show, duct-taping the principal to a wall, or teacher dares that will involve lots of students, create excitement and positive school spirit, and bring in much-needed money for your treasury. This essential resource for anyone who conducts school fundraisers also features:

• Project planning guides for organizing fundraisers

• Tips for selecting and working with vendors

• Ideas for making money through group activities

• Budgeting for events and organizations

• Pitfalls to avoid

• Fundraising resources

• Reproducible forms

• And much more!

(64 pages) $14.95 plus S/H

DVD Toolbox Series: Effective FUNdraising Learn how to plan, execute, and process fundraising activities to maximize their cocurricular compoents by providing an opportunity for many people to be involved in something significant. This class discusses the essential elements of an effective fundraising compaign and prvides a wealth of creative fundraising ideas. Based on the book, *The Bucks $tart Here: Fundraising for Student Activities*, by Lyn Fiscus and Earl Reum. Program includes one 38-minute DVD video that includes printable support/resource materials on the disc. $42.00 plus S/H

To order visit www.leadershiplogistics.us

5931585R0

Made in the USA
Charleston, SC
22 August 2010